*For Ryan and all
of our Grandkids.*

Copyright © 2020 How Steven the Bear Invented S'mores

All rights reserved. This book or any portion thereof may not be reproduced or used in any manner whatsoever without the express written permission of the publisher except for the use of brief quotations in a book review.

Published by Piper's Legacy, Inc., in the United States of America.

PIPER'S
LEGACY

First printing, 2020.

Piper's Legacy
3451 Via Montebello
192-302
Carlsbad, CA 92009

Cataloging-in-Publication Data is on file at the Library of Congress

Hardcover ISBN: 978-1-7353810-0-8

www.StevenTheBear.com

"Before we go let's make sure we have everything," said Steven.

"We have our sleeping bags. I can't wait to sleep under the stars," said Hayden.

"We have our flashlights so we can see when it gets dark," said Stella.

Lily jumped up and down and said, "We have our backpacks with snacks, cozy clothes and our toothbrushes and toothpaste."

"We have our water bottles, said Jack. "It's important to drink lots of water while we are out hiking and having fun outdoors."

"And I have our Bear Bunch flag!" said Archy. "We are all set and ready to go!"

The Bear Bunch was off on their very first camping adventure.

"We need to make sure we have lots of firewood," said Jack. "So we can cook our hotdogs and toast marshmallows."

"We also need to use a lot of rocks to make a big, safe fire pit," said Archy. "Remember what Grandpa Bear says, 'Be safe with fire OR you'll be a crier!'"

Stella pulled on Hayden's arm and said, "Why are we hanging our flag on this tree?"

"In case we get lost," said Hayden. "We can look for the flag to help us find our camp. It will also let Gigi Bear and Grandpa Bear know where we are camping when they come to meet us."

Stella held up her whistle. "Do you know why Gigi gave us these whistles?"

"Sure I do!" said Hayden. "Grandpa Bear says, 'If you're in a pickle, blow the whistle!'"

That afternoon, Steven and Jack picked juicy blueberries.

Archy fished from the dock. How many fish did he catch?

Lily practiced her birdwatching.

Hayden fed the ducks some corn that he had brought in his backpack. How many hungry ducks did he feed?

"Stella, look at those clouds. What do you think they look like?" asked Steven.

When they got back to the camp, Grandpa Bear had arrived and had made them a nice cozy fire. Gigi Bear had packed a wonderful dinner of hotdogs, macaroni & cheese, graham crackers and their favorite juice boxes. She even packed some marshmallows for dessert.

After dinner, Steven carefully roasted his marshmallow until it was nice brown and crispy, but OUCH! It was hot and stuck to his paw. "I have an idea," said Steven. He picked up one of Gigi's graham crackers and slid it under the warm sticky marshmallow. It was a perfect plate and would keep his paws clean.

As Steven was moving his backpack away from the cozy fire, a piece of chocolate he had been saving fell out and landed right on top of his marshmallow. The warm marshmallow made the chocolate soft and gooey. Steven did not know what to do. Then he thought to himself, I like graham crackers, I like marshmallows and I LOVE chocolate, maybe they would be great together. He remembered what Grandpa Bear had told him. "You don't know if you like it until you try it."

Steven picked it up and took a bite.

In fact it was SO GOOD. He wanted

SOMEMORE

and that's how Steven invented S'mores.

Steven even had enough to share with everyone.

The End!

S'more Facts

BEARS
Bears can run up to 40 miles per hour which means a bear could run the length of a football field in less than 4 seconds or the same amount of time it takes to say 4 Mississippi's.

A bear footprint or track looks like this:

FOXES
What does the fox say? Foxes have more than 40 special sounds they make.

Their footprints look like this:

RABBITS

When bunnies are happy, they jump into the air and do a special twist that is called a "Binky."

Bunnies make these kinds of footprints:

WOLVES

Wolves are born with blue eyes, but their eyes change color to yellow when they grow older.

These are what their footprints look like:

RACCOONS

Raccoons love to play during the nighttime and sleep in the daytime.

These are what their footprints, or tracks, look like:

BOBCATS

Bobcats like to spend quiet time with themselves.

Their footprints, or tracks, look like this:

BLUEBIRDS

Bluebirds have great eyesight and can see small bugs even from the tall trees.

These are their footprints:

GRAY JAYS

Gray Jays love sneaking food from campsites, that's why they are sometimes called "Camp Robbers."

These are what their footprints or tracks, look like:

S'more History

No one knows for sure who invented the first S'more. The first published recipe for "some mores" was in a 1927 publication called "Tramping and Trailing with the Girl Scouts." Credit for the recipe went to Loretta Scott Crew who made them for the Girls. To the best we know, no one has "really" ever claimed to be the inventor of S'mores.

So why not a friendly cartoon Bear named Steven?

Find Steven and the Bear Bunch online!
(With your parent's permission)

www.StevenTheBear.com

Look out for the next adventure with Steven:

Steven the Bear
Learns How to Camp

(Coming Soon)